I Can Write
Stories

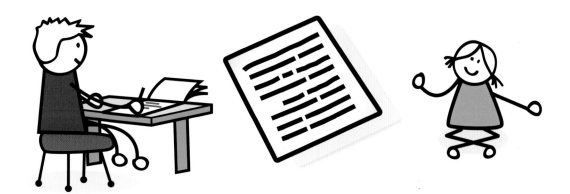

Anita Ganeri

Raintree

www.raintreepublishers.co.uk
Visit our website to find out
more information about
Raintree books.

To order:
☎ Phone 0845 6044371
📄 Fax +44 (0) 1865 312263
💻 Email myorders@raintreepublishers.co.uk

Customers from outside the UK please telephone +44 1865 312262

Raintree is an imprint of Capstone Global Library Limited,
a company incorporated in England and Wales having its
registered office at 7 Pilgrim Street, London, EC4V 6LB
– Registered company number: 6695582

Edited by Daniel Nunn, Rebecca Rissman, and Sian Smith
Designed by Victoria Allen
Picture research by Elizabeth Alexander
Original illustrations © Capstone Global Library Ltd 2013
Illustrated by Victoria Allen and Darren Lingard
Production by Victoria Fitzgerald
Originated by Capstone Global Library Ltd
Printed and bound in China by Leo Paper Products Ltd

ISBN 978 1 406 23835 8 (hardback)
16 15 14 13 12
10 9 8 7 6 5 4 3 2 1

ISBN 978 1 406 23842 6 (paperback)
17 16 15 14 13
10 9 8 7 6 5 4 3 2 1

British Library Cataloguing in Publication Data
Ganeri, Anita, 1961-
   Stories. -- (I can write)
   1. Short story--Juvenile literature.
   I. Title II. Series
   808.3'1-dc23

Acknowledgements
We would like to thank the following for permission to reproduce
photographs and artworks: Alamy pp.7 (© Tibor Bognar),
9 (© Pictorial Press Ltd); Capstone Publishers p.8 (Cynthia Martin);
Rex Features p.5 (ITV); Shutterstock pp.4 (© pjcross),
6 (© Monkey Business Images), 10 (© pat138241), 11 (© Yuri
Arcurs), 12 (© Zoran Vukmanov Simokov), 13 (© BVA), 14 (©
pichayasri), 15 (© notkoo), 15 (© yadviga), 16 (© Pushkin),
17 (© Yayayoyo), 17 (© Lindwa), 18 (© Torian), 19 (© tr3gin),
20 (© Cory Thoman), 20 (© yadviga), 21 (© Phil Holmes),
21 (© Screwy), 22 (© Nate A.), 23 (© Desiree Walstra),
24 (© blambca), 25 (© Juriah Mosin), 26 (© Rocket400 Studio),
27 (© HORUSHKIN), 27 (© laola).

Every effort has been made to contact copyright holders
of material reproduced in this book. Any omissions will
be rectified in subsequent printings if notice is given to the
publisher.

Disclaimer
All the internet addresses (URLs) given in this book were
valid at the time of going to press. However, due to the
dynamic nature of the internet, some addresses may have
changed, or sites may have changed or ceased to exist
since publication. While the author and publisher regret any
inconvenience this may cause readers, no responsibility for
any such changes can be accepted by either the author or
the publisher.

Contents

Some words are shown in bold, **like this**. You can
find out what they mean in the glossary on page 30.

What is writing?

Writing is when you put words on paper or a computer screen. It is important to write clearly so that readers can understand what you mean.

What do you like writing about?

Roald Dahl wrote stories for children and adults.

There are many different types of writing. This book is about stories. Stories are a type of **fiction**. This means that they are made up.

What is a story?

A story is a piece of writing that tells you about made-up places, people, and events. A story needs a **setting**, **characters**, and a **plot**.

Good stories can be exciting to listen to.

This man is telling a story he has learned by heart.

For many years, stories were not written down. People learned them by heart. Then they told or acted the stories out loud. This still happens in some parts of the world.

Different stories

There are lots of different types of stories. There are **myths**, fairy tales, adventure stories, **science fiction**, and animal stories. Which types of story do you like reading best?

Gulliver's Travels is an adventure story.

The story of *Thumbelina* was written by Hans Christian Andersen.

It is best to start off writing the sort of story that you enjoy reading. If you want to write a fairy tale, read lots of fairy tales written by other authors, such as Hans Christian Andersen.

Getting started

Every good story starts with an idea. Ideas may come from your imagination. You might see something funny or interesting on TV. You might remember bits of your dreams.

Where do your ideas come from?

Keep a notebook and pen with you.
Then you can jot down any ideas that
you have. Scribble down rough notes.
You can write them up properly later on.

What's the plot?

Before you start writing, you need to plan your story. Decide what happens, why, and in which order. This is called the **plot**. A plot needs to have a beginning, middle, and end.

A timeline can help you work out the plot.

Plot idea

- **Treasure ship sails across sea.**
- **Ship is attacked by pirates.**
- **Pirates steal treasure.**
- **Pirates bury treasure.**
- **Boy on holiday finds treasure.**

The beginning **sets the scene** and introduces your **characters**. The middle is where the main action happens. The end tells readers what has happened to the characters and how they solved any problems they had.

It was a wild, stormy night. The captain squeezed out the rain from his long beard.

The beginning sets the scene and grabs the reader's attention.

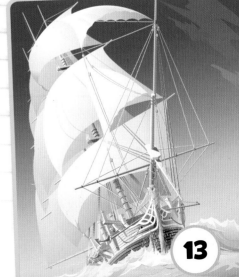

Planning a plot

Thinking up a **plot** can be tricky. Here are some tips to help you. One way is to take a word and note down anything you know about it. This is called **mind mapping**.

CASTLE

princess

fire-breathing dragon

thick walls

moat

very old

knights

This is a mind map for the word 'castle'.

Another way of mind mapping is to draw a diagram called a spidergram. Write a key word in a circle. Then write lots of connected words or ideas around the outside.

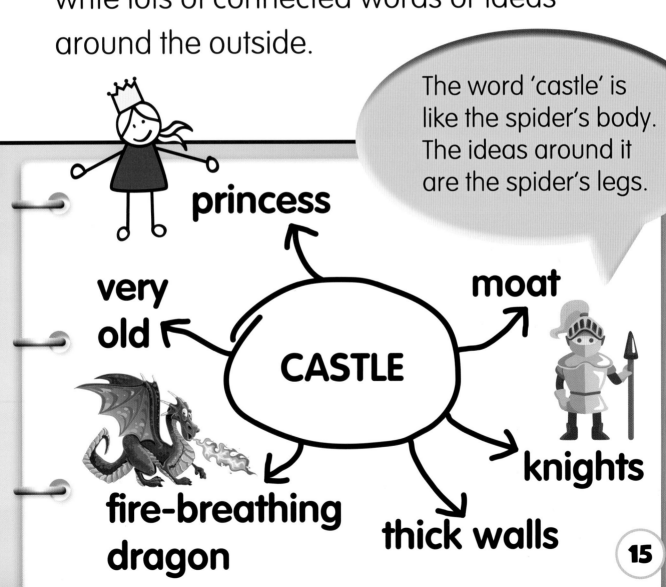

The word 'castle' is like the spider's body. The ideas around it are the spider's legs.

princess

very old

moat

CASTLE

knights

fire-breathing dragon

thick walls

Story mountain

A story mountain is another good way to plan a story. Here, you can see how it works using the famous story of Cinderella.

These are the main events in the Cinderella story.

- **Cinderella lives with the ugly sisters.**
- **The fairy godmother helps Cinderella go to the ball.**
- **Cinderella loses her glass slipper.**
- **Cinderella marries the prince.**

Draw an outline of a mountain. Then, write the parts of the Cinderella story on to it. You start at the beginning, go up the mountain, then come down the other side to the end.

Use a story mountain to work out your own **plots**.

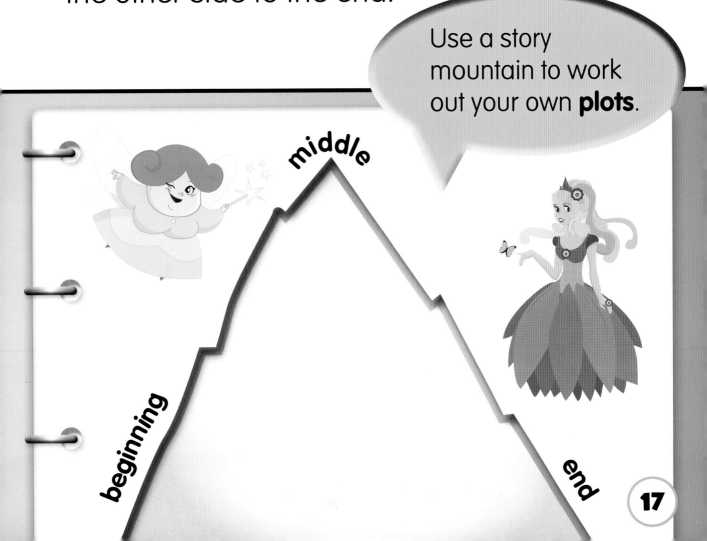

middle

beginning

end

Story setting

The **setting** is the time and place in which your story is set. It tells your reader when and where the story happens. It helps to bring your story to life.

Place: A far-off planet.

Time: Sometime in the future.

This is the setting for a **science fiction** story.

Look at the list below. You can use any of the places in the list as settings for a story. Your story may start in one setting, then move to another.

Can you think of any more settings?

<u>Possible settings</u>

train station

pirate ship

busy city

gloomy wood

supermarket

Creating characters

Make a list of your **characters**. Then note down what they look like, what sort of person they are, how they are feeling, and other interesting details.

Keep a fact file for each of your main characters.

Character file

Name: Cackle (the witch)

Age: 200 years old

Appearance: Pointed hat; straggly hair; long nose; wears a black cloak

Choose a good name for each character. It might describe what the character is like, or what he or she does. A catchy name makes a character easier to remember.

Can you match the names below with a character?

Mr Crafty	pirate
Killer Jaws	shark
One-eyed Pete	spy
Silverwings	fairy

Writing basics

You can make rough notes when you are planning your story. But write the story itself in proper **sentences** and **paragraphs** so that your readers can understand it easily.

The boy climbed high up into the tree.

A sentence starts with a capital letter. It ends with a full stop or another kind of **punctuation mark**.

A paragraph is a group of sentences. The sentences are about the same thing. Writing in paragraphs makes your writing easier to read.

The boy climbed high up into the tree. He tried to reach the kitten. It was sitting on a branch.

This paragraph has three sentences.

Writing style

Your writing style means the way you write. You can make your writing more interesting by using **adjectives** (words that describe **nouns**) and **adverbs** (words that describe **verbs**).

The big, scary monster roared loudly.

'Big' and 'scary' are adjectives. They describe 'monster', which is a noun. 'Loudly' is an adverb. It describes 'roared', which is a verb.

You can use speech to show what your **characters** are thinking and feeling. This is useful for breaking up big chunks of writing.

Speech marks (inverted commas) show that someone has spoken.

"I don't like monsters," whispered Holly.

Once upon a time...

You have done all the planning. Now it is time to start writing your story! Remember that your opening **paragraph** needs to **set the scene** and grab your reader's attention.

Jack stepped out of his spaceship and looked around. Where was he? And who were all those little green creatures?

Your opening needs to be exciting so that your readers want to know more.

Your story also needs a title. Start off with a working title. This is a title to call your story while you are writing. You can leave the final title until your story is finished.

Which of these titles would you choose for the story on page 26?

Alien Planet

Lost in Space

Starship Commander

Top tips for writing stories

1. Read lots of different kinds of stories. The more you read, the better your own writing will become.

2. Check your story through when you have finished. Make any changes you need to. Authors often rewrite a story several times.

3. Use short **sentences** to speed your story up and make it more exciting. Use longer sentences to slow it down.

4. Try to use different words, even if they mean the same thing. For example, instead of saying 'good', you could say 'brilliant' or 'amazing'.

5. Read your story out loud. It helps you to tell if it sounds right. It also helps you spot any mistakes.

6. If you can't think what to write about, choose something that happened to you. Then change some of the **characters** and details to turn it into a story.

7. Try some **automatic** writing. This is when you write down whatever comes into your head. You might be surprised.

8. Keep practising! Writing is just like riding your bike or learning to swim. You need to keep practising.

Glossary

adjective describing word that tells you about a noun

adverb describing word that tells you about a verb

automatic when you do something without thinking

characters people in a piece of writing

fiction writing that is about made-up people or things

mind mapping thinking of everything you can about a subject

myth an ancient story, often about heroes or monsters

noun a naming word

paragraph group of sentences

plot things that happen in a story and the order they happen in

punctuation mark mark you use in writing to make the meaning clear

science fiction writing about space, aliens, or the future

sentence group of words that make sense on their own

set the scene give the reader an idea of a story setting

setting time and place in which a story is set

verb a doing or action word

Find out more

Books

Getting to Grips with Grammar series, Anita Ganeri (Raintree Publishing, 2012)

How to Write Stories, Celia Warren (QED Publishing, 2008)

Websites

www.bbc.co.uk/schools/ks1bitesize/literacy

www.bbc.co.uk/schools/ks2bitesize/english/writing

Index